GU00888722

COPYRIGHT

LIMITATION OF LIABILITY

Introduction to Internet Resource Pack 1

Before working through this Internet resource pack, it is important that you read the following information that has been written to offer you guidance on how to get the best out of this resource pack.

The resource pack has been divided into units. Each unit consists of a number of IT-related categories. Throughout these categories are tasks, designed to help you understand how to use the computer and how the different parts of a computer work.

At your own pace, you are required to read through the resource pack, learning about different aspects of the computer and how it is used to connect to the Internet and 'surf' the World Wide Web.

At key moments throughout the resource pack, you will be instructed to perform a practical assignment or task. These tasks are there to help demonstrate, in a practical hands-on approach, the important theoretical aspects of the computer that might otherwise be difficult to understand merely by reading through the resource pack.

It is important that you read through each category carefully before attempting to do the tasks, as this will equip you with the knowledge you will need to answer the questions contained in each task.

Don't worry if you occasionally find yourself having to refer back to the section you have just read in order to complete a task. Only through reading each category and working on the accompanying tasks will you learn how to use the Internet to find information quickly and efficiently on any subject you like.

Consolidation exercises are also contained within each resource pack. These exercises provide yet further opportunity to re-cap on the various categories and tasks that you will have previously undertaken while working through the resource pack earlier.

The resource pack is accompanied by a supplementary pack. Carefully follow the instructions provided to ensure the appropriate use of the supplementary pack with the level one resource pack.

By following these simple instructions and correctly using this resource pack, you will find that learning how to use the Internet will be far easier and much more enjoyable.

Contents

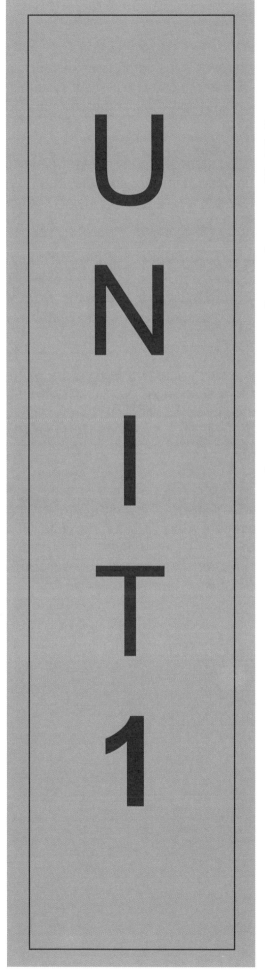

On completion of this unit you will have learnt about and practised the following:

- **An Introduction To The Internet**

- **Connecting To The Internet**

  - Hardware
  - Internet Speed
  - Opening A Web Browsing Application
  - Dial-up Connection

- **Internet Explorer**

  - The Microsoft Internet Explorer Window
  - Internet Explorer Toolbar
  - Web Addresses
  - Displaying Web Pages
  - Changing The Home Page
  - Saving A Web Page
  - Microsoft Internet Explorer Help
  - Closing The Web Browser

An Introduction To The Internet

In simple terms, the Internet is a global collection of interconnected computers transferring information via high-speed networking connections and telephone lines. It is a system of computers connected together that allows you to communicate with other people and exchange information.

There are many different ways to use the Internet, just as there are many different ways to use a telephone or fax machine. The Internet can be used to inform, educate, entertain and trade. It is possible to find information about almost every topic by using search engines to access links to thousands of relevant web sites.

A misconception about the Internet is that it is a recent development. The Internet began as an experiment in the early 1960s by the Advanced Research Projects Agency Network (ARPANET) of the U.S. Department of Defense. Its purpose was to create a computer network that would continue to function in the event of a disaster, such as a nuclear war.

Gradually, the Internet moved from a military network to a communications tool for scientists as ARPANET computers were installed at many universities within the U.S. In 1985, the National Science Foundation created NSFNET (the National Science Foundation Network), a series of networks for research and education communication. NSFNET grew rapidly as people discovered its potential and new software applications were created to make access easier.

In 1990, when the World Wide Web was officially unveiled, few people suspected how successful it would become. Even without the benefit of hindsight, it is easy to see why the World Wide Web has attracted so much attention in recent years. The World Wide Web has been heralded as a boon for education and research communities as it provides efficient and cost-effective access to a variety of information sources around the globe.

Connecting To The Internet

Hardware

Before you can access the Web, you need to be connected to the Internet. There are generally three main options of gaining access to the Internet: the company you work for or the university you are with may provide direct access. A cybercafe or public library is another option. However, the most versatile method is to use a modem to connect to the Internet from your home.

Essentially, you need the following pieces of equipment to establish a dial-up connection.

A computer - Internet Explorer (browser software) is available for PCs, Apple Macintoshes and Unix workstations, but for the purposes of this book we'll concentrate on the version for PCs running Windows. As a minimum requirement you will need a computer with a 66MHz processor, 16 Mb of RAM and 50-150 Mb of free hard disk space. A faster, more powerful computer with more RAM will make browsing the Internet quicker and ultimately more enjoyable.

A Modem - There are two types of modem: internal (one that's fitted into your computer), and external (a modem that's attached as an addition to your computer). Although modems come in a variety of speeds, anything less than 56kbps (kilobytes per second) will have you struggling to connect to the Internet. Slower modems may be cheaper, but you'll almost certainly run up a larger phone bill.

A telephone line - Most phone companies offer cheap deals on local calls, making it all the more economical to use the Internet to allocate all the information you need.

An Internet Service Provider (ISP) - A service provider has a computer system that is permanently connected to the Internet and to a 'bank' of modems. When connecting to the Internet, you use your modem to connect to one of your service provider's modems, via your telephone line, thereby making your computer (temporarily) part of the Internet.

Connection software - On your own PC, you will need to install the Dial-Up Networking utility supplied with Windows to connect to the Internet. Newer broadband systems are 'permanently connected'.

Internet Speed

Internet speed is determined by two main factors; the server capacities and the line speed of the connection to the Internet. The most common connection method for users is the Modem.

A modem is an internal or external piece of hardware connected into your computer. It links into any standard phone socket, therefore giving you access to the Internet. The word derives from **MO**dulator and **DEM**odulator.

The modem will dial your Internet access number, answer the call and will control the communication speed. Modems are available in the following speeds: 300, 1200, 2400, 9600, 14400, 28800, 33300 and 56000 kbps. Most modems are now 56 k (V90).

You may find that, when accessing certain web pages, they take a long time to display (download), and may not contain the information required. While this is happening, you are most likely to be running up the cost of your phone call. This can be mitigated with a fixed monthly tariff using freephone dial-up numbers.

When using a 56,000 Kbps (Kilobytes per second) modem to connect to the Internet, it will have a top speed of 56,000 bits per second or, in other terms, 56,000/8 = 7000 characters.

Another factor to consider when using modems is the condition of your phone line. The speeds quoted above are typical for modems in perfect condition. However, if there are any problems with your phone line (crackles etc), this can affect the connection rate and therefore the modem will work more slowly.

An alternative to connecting via a modem is to use ISDN (Integrated Services Digital Network), often known as BT Highway. This method uses your existing phone line, however it is Digital (as opposed to Analogue). The handling capacity of the ISDN line is double, as it can handle two calls at once to two different locations, as it contains two channels on the same cable.

ISDN is a faster connection than a modem at over 64,000 bps and there are no crackles as it is a digital line. Sending files over the Internet is twice as fast as using a modem.

ISDN will also connect to the Internet a lot faster than a modem. You may notice that when using a modem, it may take approximately a minute to connect. With ISDN it takes seconds.

The call charges are the same for ISDN lines. However, you should consider the installation costs involved.

Another option available when connecting to the Internet is ADSL (Asymmetric Digital Subscriber Line). This system uses digital signals down your phone line similar to ISDN. However, this system uses a 'splitter box' and splits your ordinary phone line to a high speed digital link alongside the normal phone line. The speed is faster than ISDN, at over 512,000 bps downloading and over 250,000 bps uploading. The existing phone line will work as normal.

ADSL is what is known as a 'point-to-point' system where you sign up with an ISP (Internet Service Provider) and are unable to change them. If you do decide to change them, the line has to be transferred to the new provider.

ADSL is always connected to the Internet; you will have a constant connection 24 hours per day, 7 days per week.

Opening A Web Browsing Application

To explore the Internet, you will need a software application known as a **web browser**. There are several types of web browser software available. For the purposes of this workbook you will be using **Microsoft Internet Explorer**. There are two main ways of opening Internet Explorer. Either double-click on the Internet Explorer icon on the Desktop:

Internet
Explorer

or click on the Windows **Start** button (usually at the bottom left corner of your screen), select **Programs** and then click on the **Internet Explorer** option.

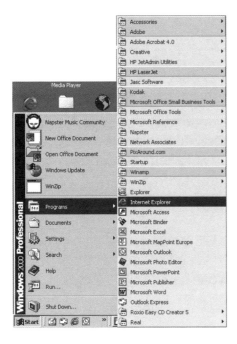

T A S K	1.	*Open Microsoft Internet Explorer.*

Dial-up Connection

As soon as you open Internet Explorer, it will attempt to connect to the Internet. If the computer you are using is part of a network or it has a permanent Internet connection, then Internet Explorer will do this automatically for you.

If the computer you are using is not part of a network or does not have a permanent Internet connection, then you might see the following screen:

This is your dial-up connection screen and it will contain the name/password details of your Internet Service Provider (or ISP). You do have the options of changing the name/password or ISP from this screen, but usually you will just have to press the **Connect** button to continue. When you've done this, your computer will attempt to connect to your ISP and if this is successful, then you will be connected to the Internet.

When you've connected to the Internet, your web browser will automatically display the browser's **Home Page**. This home page can be modified to suit your own needs and we will explain how to do that later in this unit. Below you can see a web browser displaying the Virgin Internet home page.

Internet Explorer

The Microsoft Internet Explorer Window

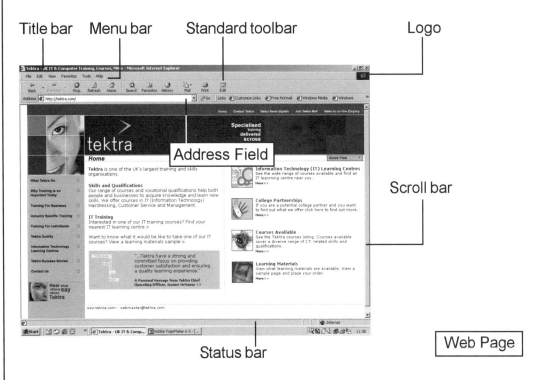

Title bar   Menu bar   Standard toolbar   Logo

Address Field

Scroll bar

Web Page

Status bar

As you can see from the diagram above, the web browser screen is divided into sections.

Title bar	This is the blue strip at the top of your browser screen. It will always show the name of the current web page.
Menu bar	The menu bar consists of drop-down menus containing commands and gives you access to all of the web browser functions, such as **Properties**, **Page Setup** and **Options**.
Standard toolbar	The Standard toolbar contains the basic commands you need to make use of the Internet.
Logo	The logo will animate while Explorer is busy searching and downloading the information on the web page.
Address field	This shows the address or URL (Universal Resource Locator) of your current web page. If you know the URL of a web page, it can be typed here.
Scroll bar	This is used to move up or down the web page.
Web page	This is the main part of your browser and it displays the current web page.
Status bar	The Status bar shows you what the browser is currently doing. For example, if a web page is still loading, you will see details of the loading process.

Internet Explorer Toolbar

Back	View the previous web page.
Forward	If you've used the **Back** button, then this will move you forward to the original page.
Stop	This will stop a web page from loading. This is useful if it's taking too long and you want to go to another web page.
Refresh	This will reload the current web page.
Home	This will take you back to the browser's home page.
Favorites	Also known as a **bookmark** because it allows you to mark or remember a certain web page and add it to your list of favourite pages.
History	This will show you a list of all the web pages that you have visited in the past in date category.
Mail	This will open up your e-mail program and allow you to send/receive mail.
Print	This will print the current web page.
Edit	This allows you to edit the existing web page.

Web Addresses

A web address is also known as a **Uniform Resource Locator** (or URL for short) and is the text that you type into the **address bar** of your web browser to display a web page. We have all seen web addresses advertised on television, in newspapers and so on, but you may not understand exactly how they work, so let's take a look at the different parts that make up a web address.

A standard web address would look something like this:

http://www.bbc.co.uk

This address consists of four parts: The protocol, the prefix or subdomain, the domain and the country code or identifier. Let's take a closer look at each of these parts.

Protocol - The protocol is the first section of the web address that reads **http://**

This defines how the data is transferred to your computer. Web pages always use a protocol called the **Hypertext Transfer Protocol** (or HTTP for short). As web pages always use this protocol, you **don't** need to type this part of the address into your web browser. Other common protocols include **ftp://** and **mailto://**.

Prefix or subdomain - This is the section that reads **www**

The prefix or subdomain is just there to help us identify what type of information is available at this web address - a prefix of **www** tells us that it is part of the World Wide Web (ie it's a web page). Other common prefixes include **mail** and **news.**

Domain - This is the section that reads **bbc**

The domain is the section that identifies the company or web page that you are looking at. Typically, the domain will match the name of the company who owns the web site, but that isn't always the case.

Country code or identifier - This is the section that reads **co.uk**

The country code or identifier will either tell you the country the web site is in or what type of person or group owns it. For example, **co.uk** means that it belongs to a **co**mpany in the **UK**. Any web address that ends in **edu** means that it belongs to a US educational establishment, **ac.uk** means that it belongs to an academic establishment in the UK, **com** is used for international commercial organisations and **gov** means that it belongs to a government department. Common country codes include **fr** (France), **de** (Germany), **it** (Italy) and **au** (Australia).

T A S K

Understanding how web addresses are constructed will help you to work out the address of any well known company/establishment. Below is a list of companies or products.

1. *Guess the web address for each of them. The answers are shown on the following page (do **not** write on this resource pack).*

    Cadbury
    Microsoft
    City University, UK
    Harvard University, US
    Federal Bureau of Investigation (FBI)
    German version of Yahoo
    BBC News
    National Geographic magazine
    UK Trading Standards
    Met Office

T A S K

The answers to the previous task are:

Cadbury - **www.cadbury.co.uk**
Microsoft - **www.microsoft.com**
City University, UK - **www.city.ac.uk**
Harvard University, US - **www.harvard.edu**
Federal Bureau of Investigation (FBI) - **www.fbi.gov**
German version of Yahoo - **www.yahoo.de**
BBC News - **news.bbc.co.uk**
National Geographic magazine - **www.nationalgeographic.com**
UK Trading Standards - **www.tradingstandards.gov.uk**
Met Office - **www.metoffice.gov.uk**

Displaying Web Pages

Now that you have looked at how the web browser works and how web addresses are constructed, let's get on the Internet and start displaying some web pages.

When you first open Internet Explorer it will display the browser's home page. To display a new page, you enter (type) the web address (or URL) into the **address bar** of the browser and then either press the **Enter** key on your keyboard or click on the **Go** button at the end of the address bar.

The following is an example of some common features to be found on a web page. Here the BBC web site has been used.

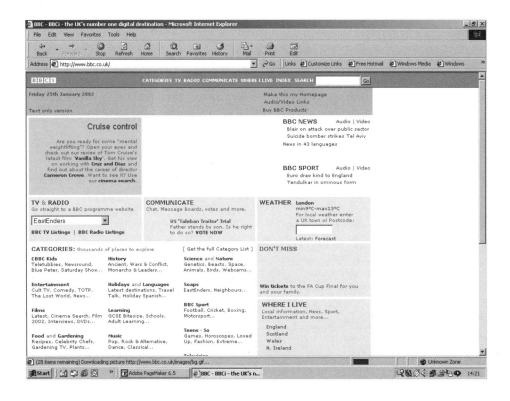

When you display a web page in the browser, you will usually be given a series of menu options that will lead to other web pages. These menu options are known as **Hypertext Links** or **hyperlinks** (usually just called **links** for short).

Any text that is underlined on a web page is usually a hypertext link to another page. In some instances the hypertext links are not even underlined.

Whenever the mouse is moved over a hyperlink on a web page, the cursor will change from its usual arrow symbol to a 'hand' symbol that looks like this.

When an image is used as a hyperlink, the image will usually highlight or change colour when you move the mouse over it, to indicate that it is a hyperlink. This effect is known as a **rollover**.

If you click on any of the underlined text, then a new web page will be opened, giving you further details on the item you selected. For example, if you wanted more information on **BBC NEWS**, then you just have to click on that option.

To get back to the main web page, you can use the **Back** button on the tool bar.

Not all hyperlinks are shown as underlined text; sometimes an image or picture can be used as a hyperlink too.

Task 01/14. Displaying Web Pages (Supplementary Pack).

Changing The Home Page

If you have a favourite web page that you want to be displayed every time you start Internet Explorer, the address can be set so that it becomes the web browser home page. To change the home page, click on **Tools**, **Internet Options** from the menu bar to display the **Internet Options** dialogue box:

The dialogue box is split into three sections; the first section, **Home Page**, displays an address box that shows the current home page.

In the example given, the home page is set to **http://www.yahoo.co.uk**. In this address box, enter the web address of your new home page.

For example, if you want the BBC home page to become your home page, then in the box you can type **www.bbc.co.uk** and then press the **OK** button to confirm. If the web page you want to use as your home page is already displayed in your browser, click on the **Use Current** button and Internet Explorer will use the current web page as your home page.

The **Use Default** button will restore the home page setting to the original address that was used when Internet Explorer was first installed.

The **Use Blank** button will give you a blank page as your home page - this is useful if you don't want to wait for a page to load every time you start Internet Explorer.

When you've set a new home page, this page will be displayed whenever you open the browser and whenever you press the **Home** button on the Standard toolbar.

Task 02/15. Changing The Home Page (Supplementary Pack).

Saving A Web Page

Web pages can be saved to be viewed/read at a later date.
To save a web page, click on **File, Save As** from the menu bar.

The **Save Web Page** dialogue box will be displayed:

Select the location to save in by clicking on the drop-down arrow and select **3½ Floppy (A:)**.

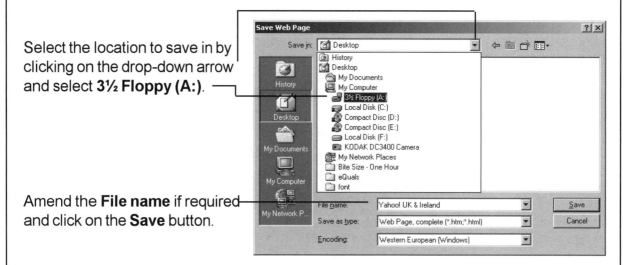

Amend the **File name** if required and click on the **Save** button.

When saving a web page in this way it will only save the text and images from the **current** web page. This means that some pages may not display correctly, as the saving process does not include special items such as rollover effects and Flash animations.

T	1.	*Open a web page in the Explorer browser window.*
A		
S	2.	*Save the web page.*
K		

To open a saved web page, click on **File**, **Open** from the menu bar and click on the **Browse** button.

Select the location where the web page was saved (for example 3½ Floppy (A:)), click on the saved web page to select it, and click **Open**.

This will enable you to view the web page 'off-line' ie not connected to the Internet.

Microsoft Internet Explorer Help

To access Help whilst using Internet Explorer, either press the **F1** key on your keyboard or select **Contents and Index** from the **Help** menu. The main help screen is shown below:

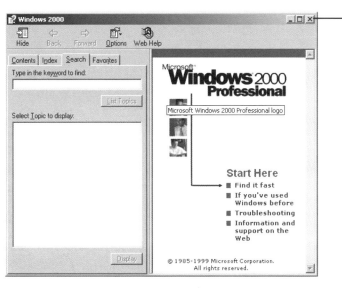

To close the screen, click on the **Close** button in the top right of the screen.

The help section is split into four categories - **Contents, Index, Search** and **Favorites**

The **Contents** section is very much like the contents section of a book and will list the main subjects that you may need help with such as Connecting to the Internet, Printing and Saving information.

The **Index** is an alphabetical list of all the items found in the help section and you can either scroll through the list to find the subject you need help on or you can type a keyword in the **Find** box and Internet Explorer will take you to that section of the index.

The **Search** section allows you to enter a word or phrase and Internet Explorer will search through all of the help files and then display all of the topics that are relevant to the word or phrase you entered. Type in a keyword, click on the list of topics or press **Enter** on the keyboard. Double-click on the topic to display the information on the right.

Favorites will allow you to save help features that have been particularly useful, for your future reference. Once you have found information on a subject area that you would like to save, by using the **Contents**, **Index** or **Search**, click on the **Favorites** tab and click the **Add** button. The subject title will then be added to your list of favourties.

<table>
<tr><td rowspan="4">**T**
A
S
K</td><td>1.</td><td>*Use the **Search** section in the help facility to find all of the topics that are relevant to the word **security**.*</td></tr>
<tr><td>2.</td><td>*Read the topic on **Understanding cookies** by searching for **cookies**.*</td></tr>
<tr><td>3.</td><td>*Use the **Index** to find out about the **lock icon**.*</td></tr>
</table>

Closing The Web Browser

To close Internet Explorer, select the **Close** command from the **File** menu or click on the **Close** button in the top right corner of your browser window.

 ———————— Close button

IMPORTANT: Depending upon how your computer has been configured, closing Internet Explorer does not necessarily close down your connection to the Internet. If you are using a dial-up connection (rather than a permanent connection or a shared connection on a network), then you may need to manually disconnect from the Internet.

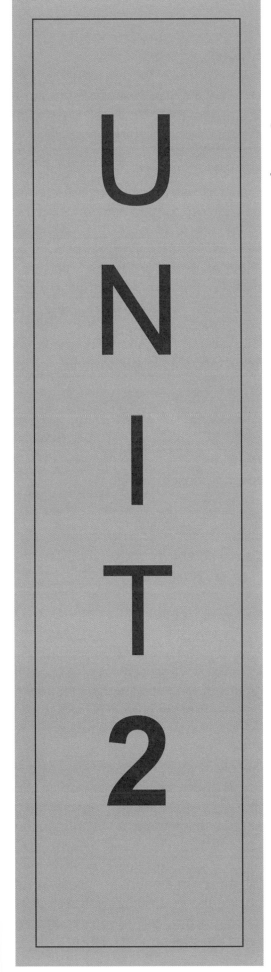

On completion of this unit you will have learnt about and practised the following:

- **ISP**

  - Selecting An Internet Service Provider (ISP)

- **Web Pages**

  - Using Page Setup
  - Printing Web Pages
  - Locating And Retrieving Saved Web Pages

Selecting An Internet Service Provider (ISP)

To access the Internet, you will need to sign up to an Internet Service Provider in the same way in which you make telephone calls using a telecoms provider. However, the choice can be a vast one and you need to consider certain factors before signing up.

An Internet Service Provider will give you a 'dial-up account'. In addition to this you will have a unique username, password and telephone number for use in accessing the Internet through their service. Special software may also be required to gain access using the chosen provider.

There are Internet Service Providers who offer free Internet access and those which offer paid-for Internet access, however it is also necessary to consider the additional services the provider may offer in relation to your requirements. Many ISP's will use a telephone number which is charged as a local rate call per minute.

Some common factors to consider when signing up to an Internet Service Provider are as follows:

- Is there a setup fee?
- What are the subscription/monthly charges?
- Does the provider have any special deals or free trials?
- Is technical support available and how much does this cost to call?
- Is technical support available at all times?
- Does the provider have a local access number?
- What will the connection speed be?
- What process is used to sign up (do I need software)?
- How many e-mail addresses will I get?
- How much web space will be available?
- Does the provider offer any on-line services or special features?
- Does the provider restrict business use?

The Internet itself is a useful resource for obtaining information regarding current Internet service providers. However if you do not have access, then many current Internet magazines will be able to assist you. Most will provide an up-to-date table of the current providers and compare all the information above.

It is worth considering exactly what you would like to get out of your service provider before signing up to one. For example, how often will you require access to the Internet? If you will only require access in the evenings and at weekends, there are special offers providing this. If you require access at all times, consider the subscription fee and the connection speed at which you can access the Internet.

There are certain providers who will offer a free trial, a certain amount of hours free of charge. After running the CD-ROM provided and using the free hours, a message is usually built into the software to ask you to start subscribing. It may ask for your credit card details. This is fine if you are happy with the service and the subsequent cost.

ISP Technical Support

Technical Support from the provider should be considered. Many providers will charge quite a fee to call their technical support team and at the time of subscribing you may not think that there will be problems. However, be aware of the call charges and when technical support is available. Some Internet Support Providers do offer technical support via frequently asked questions on their Home Page. You may have a question which has been asked and answered before.

E-mail

If you are an avid e-mail user, you may like to find out how many e-mail addresses the provider will give you; this could be unlimited amounts or a certain number. This can be useful if you have a family or more than one person requiring e-mail in your household. Also consider the software (e-mail manager) that will be used. This will usually be supplied by the provider free of charge and will be an application stored on your computer or a web based application.

Web Space

If you are considering or have already produced a web page or web site, then consider the amount of web space the provider is giving to you. If your web site contains many graphical images or applications etc, it will require more space. Most providers supply web space as part of their package.

This web space is disk storage space residing on their computers. After creating a web page or web site, and using a special piece of software called an FTP (File Transfer Protocol), your web pages can be 'uploaded' and saved in their web space. Your web site is then accessible to everyone on the Internet if they have the address (URL). Some providers are currently offering in excess of 50 Mb of free web space and some are offering unlimited space. This factor should seriously be taken into consideration if you are thinking about creating your own web site.

However, you can purchase separate Web space from independent hosting firms. This may be a more economical option.

On-line Services

With regard to On-line services, some ISP's offer much more than a simple dial up account. Once connected, their home page may have you spoilt for choice. Many have their own News updates, Chat rooms, Newsboards, Finance pages, Sport information, Entertainment news, Shopping directory, Travel services, Online Gaming, TV information etc. Some may offer a special feature, deals of free trials of software, or free access at certain times.

On making a decision on which Internet Service Provider to have your account with, the next step is to sign-up with them.

This could be as easy as making a phone call or obtaining a CD-ROM from a retail outlet. Most will have a CD-ROM as this will contain the relevant software to get you up and running on the Internet in minimal time. Software will include a 'Browser' (such as Microsoft Internet Explorer or Netscape Navigator) and an e-mail manager such as Microsoft Outlook. However, these could vary with each provider. Many providers will supply customised versions of the above software to suit their own details.

Most CD-ROMs are free, however do check as some have a very small nominal charge for the CD.

Web Pages

Using Page Setup

Before printing a web page, it is important to ensure
that the page is set to print correctly.

Click on **File**, **Page Setup** from the menu bar to view the
Page Setup dialogue box:

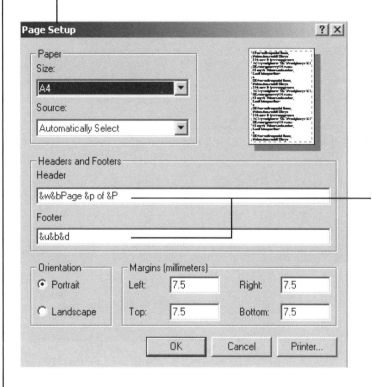

The dialogue box is split into 4
sections, **Paper**, **Headers and
Footers, Orientation** and
Margins.

Custom data can be entered
into the Header and Footer
boxes by selecting the text and
over-typing.

Paper	-	The standard paper size for the UK is A4, however by clicking on the drop-down arrow, other paper sizes can be selected. Source options will depend on the type of printer being used. It is recommended that this be left on 'Automatically Select'.
Headers & Footers	-	The Headers and Footers section determines what text will appear at the top and bottom of each page. Internet Explorer uses code to specify what is printed, such as: Window Title (**&w**) Current Page Number (**Page&p of &p**)
Orientation	-	Click to print in either Portrait (shorter edge of the paper at the top) or Landscape (longer edge of the paper to the top).
Margins	-	Margins are the area from the edge of the text to the edge of the paper. Specify custom measurements for margins here if required.

Printing Web Pages

To print a web page, use either of the methods below:

- Click on the **Print** Icon on the Standard toolbar:

  This will print all information in the web page.

- Select **File**, **Print** from the menu bar:
  This will display the **Print** dialogue box,
  providing specific print requirements.

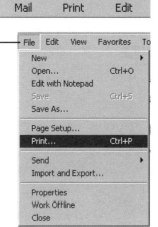

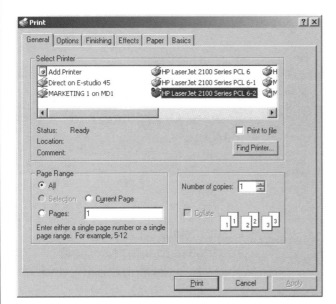

The **Select Printer** section will display an icon for the printer you are connected to.

The **Page Range** section allows you to choose whether to print all of the web page, the current page (some web pages run onto more than one page), a highlighted selection or specific pages.

The number of copies can also be specified by clicking on the up and down arrows.

Once all requirements have been selected, click on the **Print** button to print.

Task 03/24.	*Printing Web Pages (Supplementary Pack).*

Locating And Retrieving Saved Web Pages

The Internet is a huge on-line library of information and in many circumstances you may find data which you would like to save for future reference. When viewing a web page, it may contain several components such as text, graphics, links and downloadable files. It is possible to save individual components, but, depending on how the web page has been built, it may contain other hidden 'plug-ins' that will prevent you from saving this information in its entirety.

Plug-ins are small applications with added capabilities. They enhance the way web pages can be viewed in your browser. Plug-ins can be downloaded from the Internet and are available for enhancing Audio, Video and other multimedia applications.

To save a web page:

Enter the address (URL) of the web page/site in the address locator window in your browser.

Click on the **Go** button or press **Enter** on the keyboard.

Wait for the web page/site to download into your browser completely (to check this, the word '**Done**' will appear in the left-hand edge of the Status bar).

Click on **File**, **Save As** on the menu bar and the **Save As** dialogue box will appear.

Locate the **3½ Floppy (A:)** from the **Save in:** box and edit the filename if required.

Click on the **Save** button.

The web page/site has now been saved for future reference. Be aware that in most cases not only the page will be saved, but all relevant files associated with this page. These files will be stored in a folder in the same location. Note, that saving a collection of graphic - intensive pages will soon exhaust the capacity of a 3½ Floppy disk.

To Retrieve a Web Page which has been Saved:

Open the Browser.

Click on **File**, **Open** from the menu bar and the **Open** dialogue box will appear.

Click on the **Browse** button to display the **Browse** dialogue box.

Locate the **3½ Floppy (A:)** from the **Look in:** drop-down list.

Locate the web page and click on **Open**.

The web page will be displayed in the browser window. However, be aware that any changes or updates made to the web page/site on the Internet will not be displayed here.

	Task 04/25.	Locating And Retrieving Saved Web Pages (Supplementary Pack)

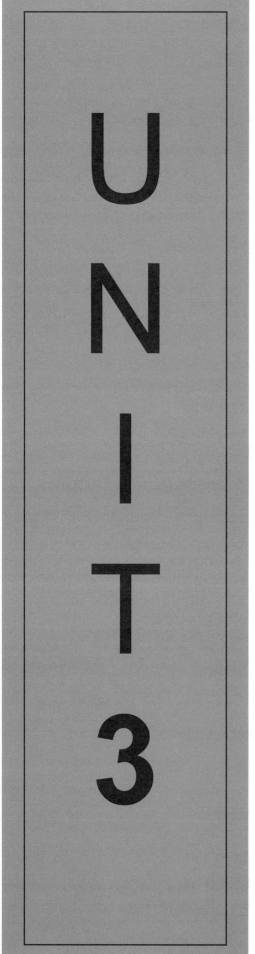

On completion of this unit you will have learnt about and practised the following:

- **Web Site Searches**

  - Browsing A Web Site
  - Performing A Defined Search
  - Using Logical Operators In Searches (Boolean)

- **Using Meta Searches**

  - Meta-search Engines
  - Bookmarking Web Pages
  - How To Move Between Selected Pages

Web Site Searches

Browsing A Web Site

In the previous section, information was gathered from the **Index** page of the web site. However, this may not be the only page in the web site, as some are made up of multiple web pages. Web pages may contain 'hyperlinks' that, when clicked, take you to another page or location within the web site.

A **hyperlink** can be identified by moving the mouse over the web page. If the mouse pointer changes to a 'hand' symbol, it can be clicked on to take you to another location in the web site.

When web sites are being constructed, the process may begin with putting together a 'Story board'. This will involve starting with the Index page and deciding on the content.

Fig.1

The content of relating pages will then be decided and these will become 'hyperlinks' on the Index page.

The example in **Fig.1** shows a possible topology (layout) of a web site (a collection of web pages).

On the browser's Home Page, move the pointer slowly over the page until you see it change into a hand icon.

If you then click with the left mouse button on the hyperlink, another page within the site will appear.

Once the new page has been opened in the browser window, press the **Back** button to return to the Home Page.

Task 05/27	Browsing A Web Site (Supplementary pack).

Performing A Defined Search

The Internet is a vast collection of web pages, with over 1 million new pages added every day. Finding the web page that you need would be almost impossible without using either an Index or an Internet search engine.

An Index is a web site that categorises the Internet. The categories can then be browsed to find the web page (or pages) of interest. An example of a popular web index is a web site called **www.yahoo.com**. Yahoo is available in many different countries and languages. The UK version of the site can be found at **uk.yahoo.com** as shown.

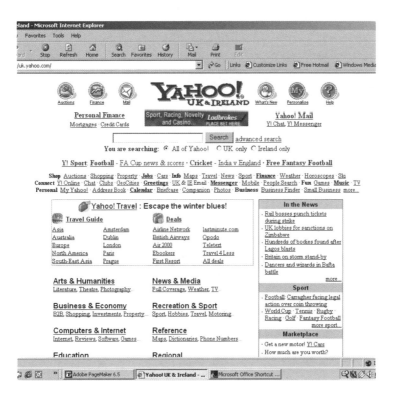

Towards the bottom of the web page, notice the main categories that Yahoo use such as **Arts & Humanities**, **News & Media**, **Business & Economy**, **Recreation & Sport** etc.

When a main category is selected, there are a series of sub-categories, which help refine a search.

Indexes like Yahoo are manually created by a team of researchers and this means that they only contain some of the most informative or most popular web sites.

There are other web sites known as search engines, which use small computer programs called **robots** or **spiders** to generate the index information. These robots and spiders automatically follow hyperlinks from one web site to the next and send indexing information back to the search engine database. Search engines tend to be much larger than indexes like Yahoo, but you have to search them using keywords rather than browsing through an index. With a keyword search, you simply enter a word or phrase and the search engine will display a summary of all the web sites that are relevant to your keyword.

The example below shows a keyword search for **ferrari**.

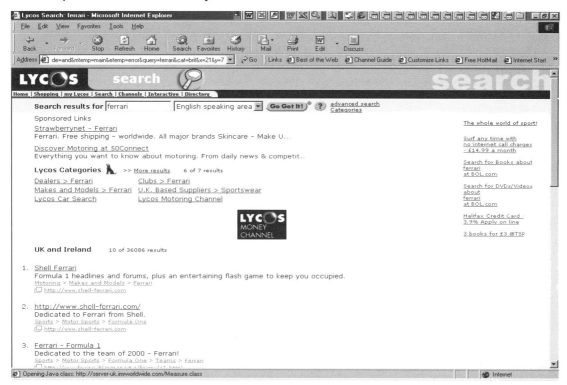

The Internet contains many different search engines. Here are some of the most well known:

Google -   **http://www.google.com**
AlltheWeb - **http://www.alltheweb.com**
Altavista -   **http://www.altavista.com**
GoTo -   **http://www.goto.com**
Lycos -   **http://www.lycos.com**
MSN -   **http://www.msn.com**

It is important to remember that the Internet is an ever-growing, constantly changing environment where web sites are being added and taken away from the World Wide Web on a daily basis. As a result, some of the aforementioned search engines may no longer be in existence. Use the search engines that are still active in order to perform the task.

None of these search engines will be able to search the entire Internet for you. So, if you are having trouble finding web pages on a particular subject, then it is worth trying another search engine, because it may include the information you are looking for.

Task 06/28.   Performing A Defined Search (Supplementary Pack).

From the task above, you will have found out that each search engine finds a different number of results and they display the results in a different order too. With a search for **Shakespeare** you may find around 1 million (or more) web pages. Obviously, you cannot possibly look through all of these pages to find the one you need, so you need to reduce the number of results by adding additional keywords.

Using Logical Operators In Searches (Boolean)

The term **Boolean** honours George Boole, a 19th Century British mathematician who suggested that logical thought could be expressed as algebra. As you will see below, it seems **logical**.

In this section, you will be using the AlltheWeb search engine found at **http://www.alltheweb.com**. Most search engines work in exactly the same way, but if you are using a different search engine, it is worth checking the Help page to see how your chosen search engine works.

Search engines use **logical operators** to help create more specific search terms. For example, the word 'Shakespeare' is used as an example again, with information required on the play Macbeth.

If both of these words were entered into the search box (ie type **shakespeare macbeth**), the search engine will display a list of all the web pages that contain the word Shakespeare **AND** the word Macbeth.

When combining two or more words in a search term, the search engine will apply the **AND** operator to them, meaning that it will only display web pages that contain all of the keywords you have entered.

You can also use the plus sign (**+**) directly in front of words that you want included in your results.

It is also possible to do the opposite of this and find web pages that contain the word Shakespeare and **NOT** the word Macbeth by typing the following search term: **shakespeare NOT macbeth**.

You can also use the minus sign (**-**) directly in front of words that you want excluded from your results.

If the search term **(shakespeare macbeth)** is entered enclosed in brackets, then the search engine will display all the web pages that contain the word Shakespeare **OR** the word Macbeth.

Search engines also support phrase searching. If a search was required for Shakespeare and his play called Romeo and Juliet, enter the following search term: **shakespeare "Romeo and Juliet"**

By enclosing Romeo and Juliet in quotation marks, it ensures that the search engine displays results that contain that exact phrase.

Task 07/30.	**Using Logical Operators In Searches (Boolean) (Supplementary Pack).**

Using Meta Searches

Meta-search Engines

When using a meta-search engine, keywords are entered which are then forwarded to many individual search engines. After waiting for a few seconds the results displayed are listed and contain all search results from all search engines. Unlike 'normal' search engines, meta-search engines do not hold a database of web pages; instead they send the search criteria to many search engines, thus providing many more search results.

This may sound like a better idea than using just one preferred search engine, as the results are larger, but bear in mind that it may not search all search engines, and therefore certain data could be missed.

If the search you perform does not provide the results required, there is often no facility to refine the search in a more advanced way.

When selecting a meta-search engine to use, consider the following factors:

*   How many and which search engines will it search from a single search box?
*   Does it cost anything?
*   How are the results consolidated (are they in a clear and concise readable format)?
*   What is the search ability, ie can you input phrases, boolean searches etc?
*   Is there a Help facility, and how effective is it?
*   Does it work with the browser you are using?

To perform a meta-search, first enter the address (URL) of the meta-search engine.

In this example www.profusion.com has been used. The Keyword entered is 'Fishing'.

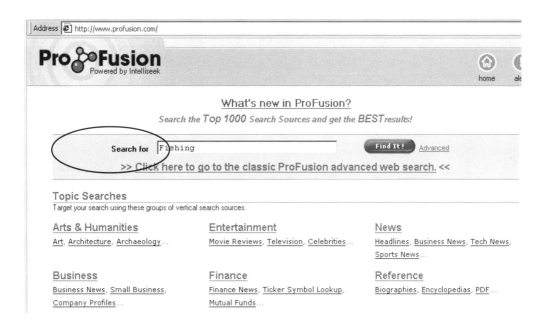

Click on the **Find It** button and the meta-search engine will search many other search engines and display a list of results as below:

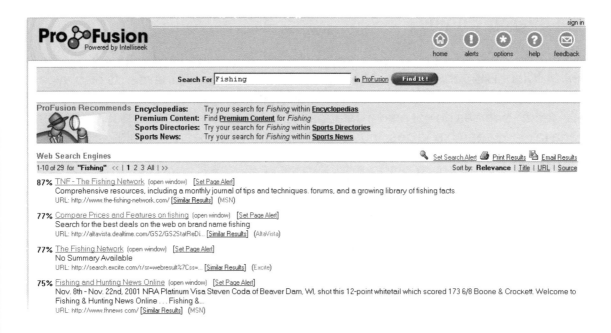

To visit any of the sites listed, click on the link. Notice that the name of the search engine the web site is registered with is also displayed.

Some meta-search engines offer additional services such as **Search Alerts** and **Page Alerts**. A Search Alert will perform the search again on subsequent days to give you up-to-date information automatically. This information will then be e-mailed to you. A Page Alert will advise you of changes to a certain web site/page as they can be updated regularly.

If you prefer not to use keywords to search, the directory of categories can be used on the Home Page. Click on the **Home** button to navigate back to the categories available.

If the meta-search engine chosen can perform advanced searches, you may have the option to eliminate or add certain search engines to the list.

Bookmarking Web Pages

A favourites or bookmarks list keeps track of the locations on the web you wish to return to. You can add pages that you intend to visit frequently to a favourites list. This stores your favourite web sites/pages for easy access and for future reference.

Enter any URL address from any of the previous exercises into the address bar on your web browser and press **Enter** on your keyboard.

To add the site you are currently viewing to your Favourites list:

Click on **Favorites** on the menu bar and select **Add to Favorites**.

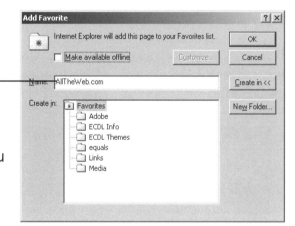

You can personalise the name of the site to something more memorable, or something shorter. Click **OK**.

You can now return to this page whenever you wish by simply selecting it from the Favorites list on the main menu, where it has now been included.

To recall a web site from your favourites list, select **Favorites** from the menu bar. Select the web site address required.

To delete items from your favourites list, select **Favorites** from the drop-down menu. Click on **Organise**, click on the web site address you wish to delete and press the **Delete** button.

Task 08/33.	Bookmarking Web Pages (Supplementary Pack).

How To Move Between Selected Pages

Sometimes we will want to return to pages we have recently viewed and then move forward to return to more recently seen pages. There are two convenient ways to do this:

(a)   Use the toolbar **Back** and **Forward** buttons
(b)   Make a direct selection of the relevant URL listed in order of access in the **Address** drop-down box

Imagine you have been surfing a site about parks and playing fields and have clicked on links and hotspots within the site and you wish to return to a previous page. The easiest way is to click the left-pointing arrow in the toolbar to page **Back**.

If you wish to return to the page before going back, click on the right-pointing **Forward** arrow.

If you wish to return several pages or sites back through the surfing session, it may be inconvenient or even impossible to access the desired page using **Back**. Instead you can use the **Address** bar.

To access the **Address** bar click on the drop-down arrow at the right side of the bar to view the list of sites visited. Select the site you wish to revisit and it will appear on your screen.

NB   Other ways such as the **History** button can also be used to visit previous sites and will be covered in the next level course.

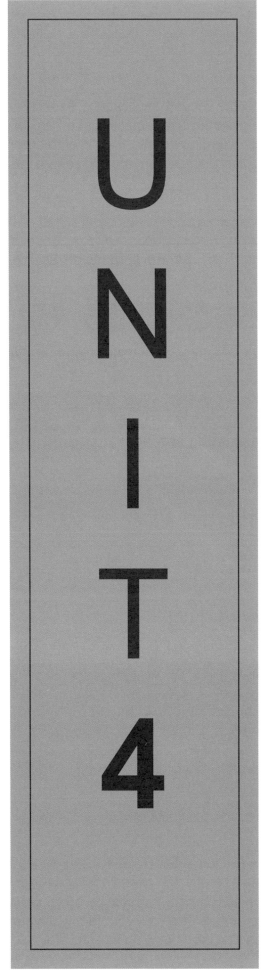

On completion of this unit you will have learnt about and practised the following:

- **Security**

  - Internet Security
  - Ways In Which Viruses Are Distributed
  - Anti-virus Software
  - Password Protection
  - Encryption
  - Firewalls
  - Backing Up

- **Copyright**

  - Copyright And The Internet
  - Health And Safety For Microcomputer Users

Security

Internet Security

When accessing the Internet, it is important to consider the security implications, especially with services such as Internet banking and shopping readily available. As soon as you make a connection to the Internet, your computer is exchanging information with other computers across the Internet. You will need to consider how safe, private and secure this is and what measures can be taken to reduce the risk of theft.

This unit explores some of the main security issues regarding accessing the Internet and the reasons why preventative measures should be taken. Security does, however, depend on which sites you visit and what browser software you use. For the purpose of this unit, Microsoft Internet Explorer Version 5.5 is used.

To access Microsoft Internet Explorer's security settings:

Click on **Tools**, **Internet Options** from the menu bar and select the **Security** tab; the following dialogue box will appear:

Please do not change any of the existing settings!

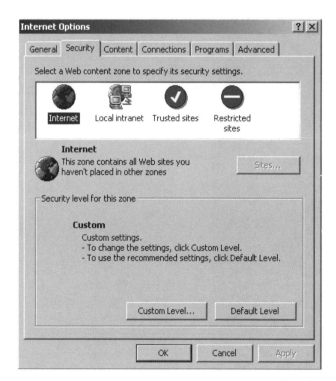

Within the security options, web sites can be categorised into one of four 'security zones': local Intranet zone; trusted site zones; Internet zone or restricted sites zone. A level of security can be added to each zone, ie low, medium or high. Security can also be customised if required. The reason for setting such security is to ensure that you, your family or your business only access trusted web sites, and reduces the risk of viewing harmful sites.

Whenever you attempt to access a web site, the software will first check the security settings to see which zone is applied.

The four security zones:

Internet Zone	-	Contains anything which is not on your computer or an Intranet or assigned to any other zone. The security level for this zone is Medium.
Local Intranet Zone	-	Local Intranet sites are usually company web sites, which are viewed by employees internally. Sites can be added to this zone if required. The security level is Medium.
Trusted Sites	-	Contains sites you trust, therefore you are confident that, when accessing this site, it will pose no threat to your computer. Sites can be assigned to this zone. The default security level for this zone is Low.
Restricted Sites	-	Contains sites you do not trust, or sites of which you are unsure. Sites can be assigned to this zone. The default security level for this zone is High.

The security level for each zone can be changed, ie if you would like to change the Trusted Sites security level to Medium, this is possible.

To ensure your time accessing the Internet is safe and protected, it is worth considering the factors that will make this possible.

Computer security may not be at the forefront of your mind when you want to access information fast, but this could save you time in the long run. Think of the security of your computer as a 'protective brick wall' which is made up and built with lots of small brick components. The more components contained in the wall, the safer your computer will be against a security breach.

Some of the most common aspects regarding security are:

- Protection against virus attacks
- Password protection
- Software security settings
- Firewalls
- Backing up

Ways In Which Viruses Are Distributed

Viruses are self-propagating computer progams designed to intrude.

Viruses can be transmitted by any route that transfers data between computers' storage media. The two principal routes are via:

(a)   Disk Transfers
      Viruses traditionally nestle in the boot sectors of disks, especially transferable system disks. They secretly transfer to the boot sectors of the transferee system when infected files are copied across. Nevertheless, viruses can infect any file and may be introduced without wholesale disk copying.

(b)   Net Transfers
      Viruses can travel through the public telephone system during downloads from the Internet. Infection from web pages is possible but relatively rare. Systems are more vulnerable to FTP downloads and especially to viruses conveyed by e-mail attachments.

The key defence is regular file backup and prevention is by the use of firewalls and other active anti-virus monitoring software. Regularly updated anti-virus packages are also capable of removing or neutralising some existing virus infections.

Anti-Virus Software

Every computer should be running up-to-date anti-virus software. Preferably one should be used that will scan any files which are being downloaded to your system or which have been sent to you via e-mail, as this is where many viruses are aimed and how they are spread to others.

It is important to have up-to-date software of this type as new viruses are being written every day. The more up-to-date your software is, the better the chance of cleaning the infected files. After all, prevention is better than cure in this case. For more information on viruses, types of virus and how they spread, see the section on Computer Viruses.

<u>Password Protection</u>

Passwords are used in various circumstances, not only on the Internet, but can be used in the everyday working environment to gain access to your computer. If you visit certain sites, you may be asked to 'sign-up', or 'create an account', in which case you will be supplied with a username and password (or you may pick one yourself).

It is very tempting to create a straightforward password of a certain amount of characters, and which relates to someone or something in your life. However, passwords are being cracked and therefore a longer and more unfamiliar password is recommended instead. The key is to make the password longer than 4-6 characters and to mix letters with numbers, also with punctuation marks such as a hyphen.

Some recommendations for creating a password are as follows:

- Do not use a common word which directly relates to you and your family.

- If possible, mix lowercase and uppercase characters, such as 'weAthER'.

- Use passwords with a minimum of 6 characters, mixing letters and symbols.

- Use different passwords for sites visited or accounts held, therefore if one password is cracked, they will not automatically have the password for all other private accounts you have on the Internet.

If you have numerous passwords for use on the Internet, try not to display them in a place where they can be easily seen by anyone using your computer (ie next to your computer)! If you really need to have them written or recorded, keep them in a safe place away from your computer.

Software Security Settings

As discussed in the earlier section, using Microsoft Internet Explorer's security settings can be applied by selecting **Tools**, **Internet Options** and clicking on the **Security** tab. The settings available will depend on the browser software being used. It is well worth checking your browser's capability with regard to security.

Other security settings with regard to the Internet are **Certificates**. These are of particular use when you are about to send your credit card details over the Internet to make a purchase etc.

If you are interested in Internet shopping but are worried about the security issues, Microsoft Internet Explorer has a facility accessible by clicking on **File**, **Properties**, **Certificates**, whilst viewing the web page/site in question. This will display the web site certificate (if the site has one) which is an on-line document which verifies the site's identity. You will therefore know that the information you send is going to the correct place.

There are two types of certificate: a **personal certificate** and a **web site certificate**. A personal certificate is designed to protect your identity over the Internet. They control the use of your own identity by having a 'private key' which is known only to you on your system. When this key is used with mail applications, they are also known as **Digital IDs**.

Security certificates (whether personal or web site) work by being associated with a 'public key'. Only the owner knows the matching 'private key' that will allow the owner to 'decrypt' or make a **digital signature**.

The **digital signature** part of the security certificate is an 'electronic identity card'. It tells the recipient that the information is valid and that it is directly from you and has not been interfered with.

Security certificates are issued by independent certification authorities and there are different levels of security certificate.

If a **Lock** icon appears, the site is a secure one and automatically sends you its security certificate.

If you are about to send your details to an unsecured site, a message may appear advising you of this, and ask if you would like to continue.

Encryption

Encryption is used by on-line banks to protect the information and data contained in any transactions made over the Internet. Information is exchanged between the Bank's computer system and your computer system. Before this exchange takes place, the information or data is converted into code. When it reaches the destination, it is decoded. The reason for this is to protect your data from being intercepted and read. If this was attempted, the data would not appear in a readable format due to the encryption applied.

To check that encryption is being used on a site, check the status bar. If using Microsoft Internet Explorer, a **Lock** icon will appear. There are two levels of encryption, the difference being the number of keys it would take to crack the code. There are 40-bit encryption and 128-bit encryption levels and single key and dual key crytographic modes.

To check a web site's level of encryption:

Click on **File**, **Properties**, **Certificates** whilst viewing the page to be checked.

Select **Encryption type** in the **Fields** box.

Information regarding the page's encryption will appear in the **Details** box.

Click on **Close** and **OK** when complete.

Firewalls

A firewall is a piece of software which is similar to the 'brick wall' theory about security settings as a whole. It will enable you to access the Internet freely, but there will be certain restrictions on data and information coming in the other direction, ie from the Internet to you.

A firewall will act as a shield, protecting everything you have on your computer. Firewall software has the ability to provide you with an **Alert**, which is a signal to advise you that someone is trying to break into your system to access your personal data.

Backing Up

The main reason for making a backup of your data and information contained on your computer is to protect yourself against sudden computer problems such as a hard disk crashing or a virus that has deleted all system files, making you unable to access your data. Theft is another important factor and this is why you should make regular copies of your data and store it in a safe place.

There is special software available for backing up data. However, you should use a removable source such as floppy disk or CD-ROM to backup data.

Copyright

The Copyright, Patents and Registered Designs Act covers copyright. Copyright is a right of authors to prevent unauthorised copying or exploitation of their work for a limited period of time. Areas affected by copyright are: literary, dramatic, musical, artistic and graphical works.

Copyright is generated automatically when work is created. Copyright lasts for the life of the author, plus 50 years from the end of the calendar year in which the author dies. It is a right to protect unauthorised copying of an original work. All copyright work should be marked with the International Copyright Symbol © or with the word 'Copyright', the name of the owner and the date or year the work was carried out, for example:

© Tektra 2002

However, unmarked copy must still be presumed copyright.

Copyright And The Internet

It is a temptation when visiting web sites to copy or take copies of certain information contained within them, such as images, text, photographs and even the code they have been written in. However, all of this work is protected by copyright. If you would like to use any material which appears on a web site, permission must be sought from the owner of the site first.

Information can only be copied from the Internet if it falls under one of the following categories:

*   It has been created by federal government.
*   The copyright has expired.
*   The copyright has been abandoned.

Some web sites will give permission for the information, graphics or photographs etc to be used elsewhere. However, you are not entitled to claim the copyright on this material, as you are not the original owner. You can still display the copyright symbol on the material, although this will apply to the data created by yourself only. A small piece of text should be added to advise that certain aspects have been used based on permission from the owner.

Task 09/40.	Consolidation Exercise.

Health And Safety For Microcomputer Users

It is undoubtedly the case that there are many health risks associated with computers, though our experience with other industrial tools suggests it will be decades before we feel their nastier effects.

In the meantime, stick to these common sense principles:

(a)   Never spend more than **two hours** at a stretch in front of a screen. Take a walkabout break of at least fifteen minutes.
       Spend less than **four hours a day** in front of the screen, using the other time for pencil-and-paper preparation or other tasks.

(b)   Closely monitor the speed and amount of your **keyboard work**, especially if you are a professional typist. Habitual, high-speed typing is known to cause Carpal Tunnel Syndrome, a crippling premature arthritis.

(c)   Abandon flickering or other faulty screens and report them to someone in charge.

(d)   Adjust the brightness and contrast of your screen to your own needs. Keep the screen clean. Position it away from the glare of the sun or internal lighting.

(e)   Position your manuscript copy to avoid neck strain - in an adjustable copyholder, for instance.

(f)   Adjust your chair to lend lumbar support (to the small of the back) and to support the body in such a manner as to prevent slumping or slouching.

(g)   Never attempt to balance keyboards or other devices on your lap.

(h)   Use wrist supports and foot rests where desirable. But do not let them encourage excessive machine attendance.

(i)   Make sure the work room is air-conditioned, or at least well ventilated.

(j)   Never remove a machine's cabinet or part of its fairings when it is connected to the electric supply. Never attempt to remove a trapped diskette without unplugging the drive or the computer that houses that drive.

(k)   Never eat, drink or smoke in the presence of a machine.

(l)   Never push, play or 'horse around' near a computer, or any other electrical or mechanical device.

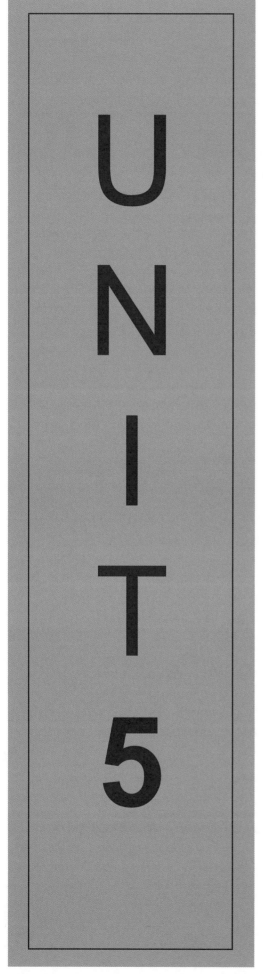

On completion of this unit you will have learnt about and practised the following:

- **Internet Ups And Downs**

    - Typical Services Available Over The Internet
    - Terminology Associated With The Internet

©Tektra TEKIE1RP1102

Internet Ups And Downs

Typical Services Available Over The Internet

The Internet is not only a source of reference or an on-line library, it also offers useful services to the public.   The services offered are designed to save you time and money by performing everyday tasks 'on-line' such as banking and shopping instead of having to leave the house or office.

Internet banking

All major banks and building societies have their own web site and many offer Internet banking in addition to this. This means that you can take advantage of their services without having to enter a branch, like opening an account or getting a credit card. The bank will usually offer an incentive to performing these actions on-line, which can be in the form of special interest rates or free of charge facilities on accounts.

Many banks may go one step further and offer special software to allow you to take care of your own money 'on-line'. This means that you can view your account transactions and transfer money from one account to another. The bank will use 'secure' connections to protect your privacy and may use a 'username' and 'password' facility. There are certain banks which offer 'on-line' banking only, ie they have no branches on the high street. Always research the services available in this area before signing up.

Shopping

Shopping via your computer can seem like the ideal way to shop, ie no traffic jam, queues, crowds or parking problems. There are thousands of web sites now offering shopping services, many of which offer the incentive of discounts for shopping on-line. Many organisations are high street stores too, and some are on-line only.

Whilst some people are totally confident in shopping via the Internet, there is still a percentage of the public who have fears. If you have not experienced this service you should visit the Office of Fair Trading web site for advice and information regarding your rights as a consumer and member of the public (http://www.oft.gov.uk/html/shopping/).

If you are confident in entering debit and credit card details onto your computer, then Internet shopping can work for you. Many of the well known stores who have high street branches will offer a secure connection/site.

Shopping services include: holidays, food and drink, organic products, frozen food, flights, books, music, video and DVD, computers and computer products, flowers, cars, electrical goods etc.

An alternative shopping service available is **On-line Auctions**. There are many sites now offering this service. Items are put on-line for auction by organisations or the general public and are bidded for. The highest bidder wins the item.

TV and Radio

The Internet gives you access not only to information on TV and radio listings but also to those broadcasts which are not available through your conventional TV or radio.

It is possible to listen to radio stations around the world through your computer via the Internet if you have the correct applications installed, together with the hardware which makes it possible, such as speakers and a sound card.

To view TV or listen to radio, a technology called 'streaming' is used. A signal is being run to your computer as you are watching or listening. However, to achieve this you may need to install plug-ins first. Plug-ins such as Flash and Shockwave are for use with Video and Audio.

In addition to plug-ins, you will require software too enabling you to view and play your programs. A common application used for this is Realplayer. There are others such as Windows Media Player and QuickTime.

When considering using the above services, check your computer's specification first, ie has it the ability to handle this much data? There is a lot of information being sent to your computer in a streaming broadcast and it is being downloaded to your hard disk in 'packets' of data. Your computer will handle this large amount of information by 'buffering'; this means that the computer is setting aside a temporary storage area in the computer's memory to receive and store the information being sent. It will then rebuild the data into the images and sound you require.

If images and sounds are not appearing or sounding correct, this may be due to your computer's processor or the telephone connection being used. Other factors can include Internet traffic.

With regard to specifications, you may only require a soundcard and speakers to take advantage of this service. However, it is possible to turn your computer into a TV using an additional 'card' added to the computer. This will allow your computer to receive TV signals via a TV aerial cable, which will therefore appear live on the monitor, whereas you would normally be viewing an Internet broadcast.

The graphics card in your computer will control the image quality on the screen. Computers will have one, but these are upgradable if required.

To enable the use of camcorders and other video equipment, a video capture card can be installed to enhance video sequences.

To check your computer's specification, ensure that you have a 486 or higher processor, Microsoft Windows 95 operating system or higher, a soundcard and speakers, a 56Kbps modem or higher and a connection to the Internet.

Education and Training

The Internet can be a useful resource for gaining information regarding education and training. There are sites available to teachers, parents, adult learners, students and children.

Services offered are vast, and include: help on exam revision, news articles, employment opportunities, resource materials, downloadable files for use in education, study aids, useful contacts, help and advice, on-line learning, studying abroad, finding the right school, college and university information and careers advice.

News and current affairs

Some current news is posted onto the Internet. The news is always readily available and up to date. An advantage of getting the latest news from the Internet is that it may go into more detail than a conventional news programme. You also have the ability to view/read information about the news which interests you and you only. News sites include BBC News (www.bbc.co.uk/news), which is a reliable source of quality researched new items. The site also contains audio and video links on topics.

There are several 'ticker services' available via the Internet. This is where a small window (most often a bar) will place itself somewhere on your computer desktop. This small window or bar will display the latest news headlines in a scrolling effect. If you see a particular news item of interest, you can click on the story to view the article. Tickers will need to be installed onto your computer, but they take only minimal time and are very straightforward. Some will give you the ability to select which categories of information to receive.

The Internet also offers the advantage of giving you access to news from around the world and sites such as www.cnn.com and www.sky.com/news are particularly useful.

Other Internet services include:

Arts and Entertainment, Finance, Travel, Food and Drink, Computers, Health and Fitness, Lifestyle and Fashion, Hobbies, Science and Nature, Cars and Bikes, Sport and Children's sites.

Task 10/47. Consolidation Exercise.

Terminology Associated With The Internet

While using the Internet, it is inevitable that you will encounter specialised words or phrases that are used when describing various features and functions associated with the net.

The following acronyms and web-specific terms are an attempt to decipher some of the jargon used and to provide a better understanding of how the Internet works.

- **e-mail**   Short for electronic mail, e-mail is the Internet's equivalent of letters and faxes.

- **FTP**   File Transfer Protocol (as its name might suggest) is the method of moving files from one location to another over the Internet.
FTP sites are simply a large collection of files (like a library) on a particular subject area.

- **WWW**   This stands for the World Wide Web, which is part of the Internet.

- **HTTP**   Hypertext Transfer Protocol is the system that is used to transfer web pages from the Internet to your computer.

- **HTML**   Hypertext Markup Language is the language used to write web pages for the Internet.

- **URL**   Uniform Resource Locator is the technical term for an Internet address, ie www.tektra.com

- **Browser**   This is the piece of software that you need before you can access the World Wide Web. Microsoft's Internet Explorer is the browser on your computer that is used to view web pages.

- **ISP**   Internet Service Providers enable you to connect to the Internet via a modem and a telephone line.

- **Home page**   This is the first page the browser will open when you are connected to the Internet.

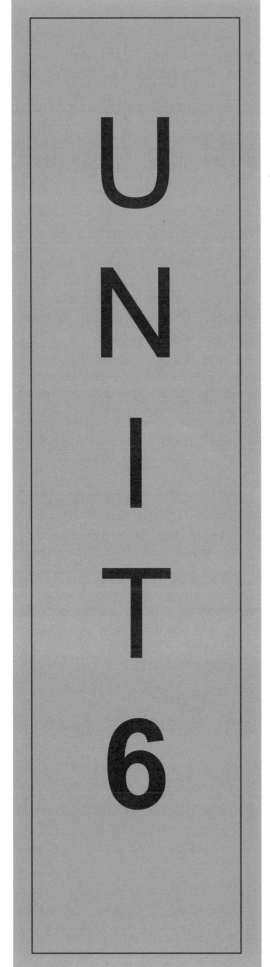

On completion of this unit you will have learnt about and practised the following:

- **E-mail**

    - Using An E-mail File Management System
    - Electronic Mail
    - Opening An Electronic Mail Application
    - The Folder List
    - Using The Inbox
    - Opening A Mail Message
    - Microsoft Outlook Express Help

- **Messages**

    - Creating E-mail Messages
    - Sending E-mail Messages
    - Retrieving E-mail Messages
    - Reading E-mail Messages
    - Deleting E-mail Messages
    - Forwarding E-mail Messages
    - Opening Attached Files
    - Attaching Files To E-mail Messages
    - Saving E-mail Messages
    - Printing An E-mail
    - Shutting Down The E-mail Program

E-mail

Using An E-mail File Management System

To use e-mail effectively, an application called an e-mail manager is used. Essentially there are two types of e-mail account: user-based accounts such as those supplied by your ISP (Internet Service Provider) and web-based accounts such as those offered free of charge by Internet web sites like **Hotmail** or **Yahoo**. For the purposes of this workbook, Microsoft Outlook Express is used. E-mail management applications determine the way in which your e-mail messages are handled and stored.

Electronic Mail

E-mail stands for 'electronic mail' and is the Internet's version of sending letters and faxes. Using e-mail is both quicker and cheaper than using either letters or faxes, but more importantly it allows you to attach files to your message. This means you can send ordinary text documents, as well as pictures, sound samples and video clips.

You can send an e-mail to anyone who has an e-mail account on the Internet. However, you will need to know their e-mail address to send them a message. An e-mail address is generally structured like the example below:

jack@hotmail.com

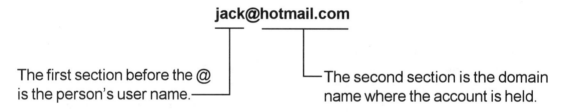

The first section before the @ is the person's user name.

The second section is the domain name where the account is held.

Open An Electronic Mail Application

To use e-mail effectively, an application called an e-mail manager is used. For the purpose of this workbook, Microsoft Outlook Express is used. E-mail management applications determine the way in which your e-mail messages are handled and stored.

To open the application:

Click **Start**, **Programs**, **Outlook Express**.

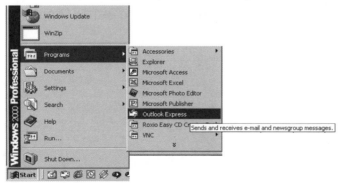

The **Outlook Express Window**, similar to that shown over the page, will now be displayed.

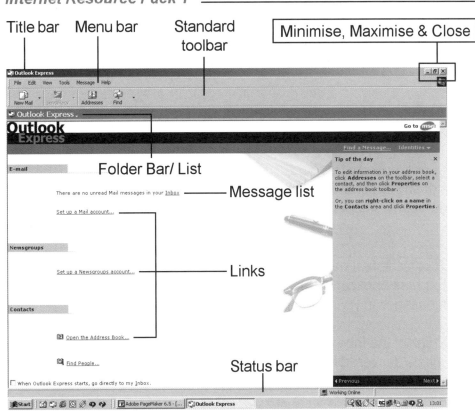

Title bar	Displays the name of the application and the current folder selected. The Minimise, Maximise and Close buttons also appear on the title bar.
Menu bar	A selection of drop-down menus containing commands.
Toolbar	A bar containing buttons (icons). The buttons perform commonly used commands when pressed.
Folder bar	Displays the current folder.
Status bar	Displays information such as how many new messages have been received.
Folder list	When clicked, displays the list of available folders.
Message list	Displays all messages contained within the selected folder.
Links	Hyperlinks to other features within Outlook Express.

T A S K	1.	*Open Microsoft Outlook Express and familiarise yourself with the window.*

The Folder List

To display the contents of any folder, click to select it. The contents will be viewed in their own window, divided into an upper and a lower pane.

Outlook Express This is the first page you arrive at once you open the Outlook Express application. Here you can see the number of unread messages in your Inbox.

Inbox Think of the Inbox as your 'letterbox'. All new e-mail messages will be delivered here.

Outbox All your sent messages are contained in this folder, ready to be 'posted' once you connect to the Internet.

Sent items This folder contains all the messages that have been sent.

Deleted items Any messages deleted from the Inbox are sent to the Deleted Items folder. This acts as a safeguard against accidental deleting. The messages are permanently deleted if you delete them from here.

Drafts Saving a message as a draft means that you can edit this message at a later date and send it on to another recipient.

Contacts Like a personal diary or contact book, you can list the names, details of colleagues and business contacts, to be retrieved for future reference at the click of a button.

Using The Inbox

When you receive an incoming e-mail message, it will appear in your Inbox. New messages appear in bold to show that they have not been read. Once a message has been read, the bold will disappear. The example below shows an unread message and how it appears after being read.

If the Inbox contains new mail messages, it will appear bold, together with a number in brackets. This number is the quantity of unread messages contained in the Inbox.

The Standard Toolbar

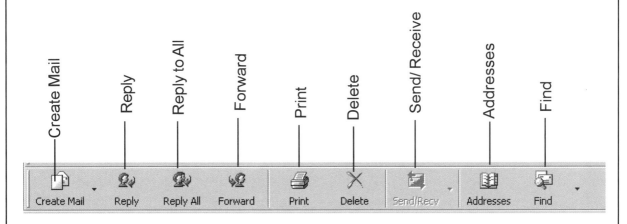

Opening A Mail Message

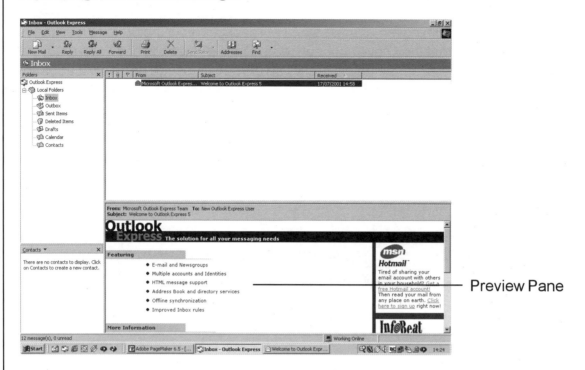

Preview Pane

To open a mail message, click to select it. The message will appear highlighted (as above). If you have the Preview Pane displayed, the message contents will appear here. Alternatively, to open the message, either double-click the message (recommended) or click on **File**, **Open** from the menu bar.

The message will appear in its own window:

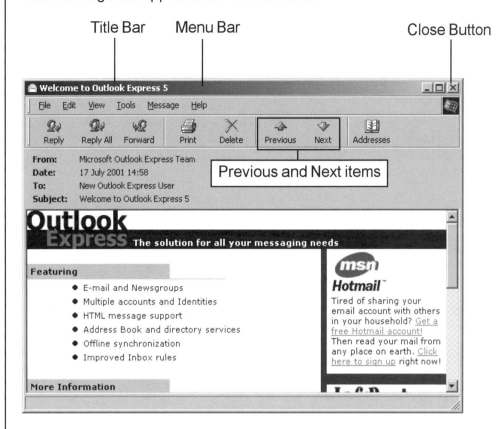

The message subject will appear on the title bar of the message window.

The message contains its own menu bar and toolbar.

By selecting the **Previous** and **Next** buttons, other messages in the selected folder can be read.

The message also gives useful information such as who the message was from; the date and time it was sent; who it was to; and the subject. Other information, such as whether the message was sent with High Priority, will appear if this option was activated at the time of sending it.

To close the message window once read, click on the cross at the top right of the window (the **Close** button).

Microsoft Outlook Express Help

If you require assistance at any time whilst using Outlook Express, use the **Help** command.

Click the **Show/Hide** icon to the left of the toolbar to show the **Content/Index/Search** window.

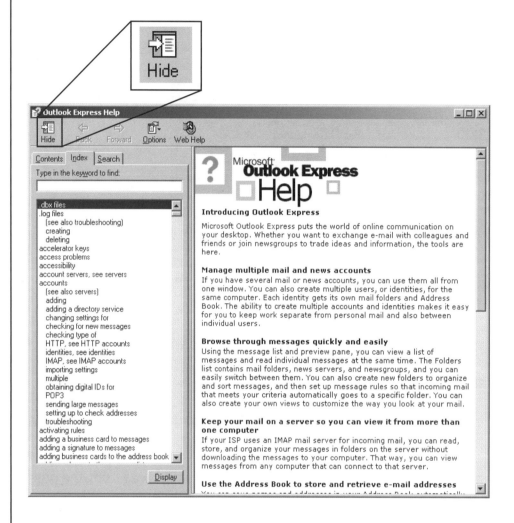

To display any of the topics in the **Contents** section, click to select them. If an icon of a book appears to the left of the topic on selecting, other topics are listed in this section.

The topic details will appear in the right window.

If you are looking for something specific, either use the **Index** or the search facility. The **Index** allows you to input a word or phrase and check if this appears in the list. When the word appears, click to select the subject to reveal **Help**.

The **Search** tab allows you to input a word or phrase and search for all related items of that word.

Another method of getting help when performing a task in Outlook Express is to press the **F1** key on the keyboard. This will display **Help** and information on the task in hand.

Messages

Creating E-mail Messages

To create a new mail message, use either of the methods below:

Click on **File**, **New**, **Mail Message** from the menu bar, **or**

Click on the **Create Mail** button on the toolbar.

This will activate a new message window for your message:

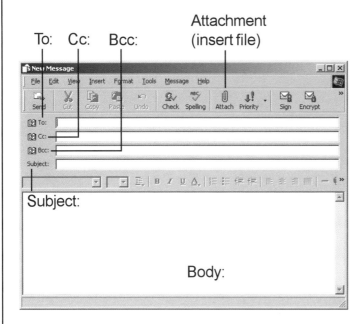

Sending E-mail Messages

When sending an e-mail, there is a header to every message that contains the following details:

To: In this space, you enter the e-mail address of the person you want to communicate with. This person is normally called the recipient.

Cc: There may be recipients who you want to copy the message to. This is the space used for the carbon copy.

Bcc: Other recipients of the message will not see the name of the recipient in the blind carbon copy text area.

Subject: This section is used to type a subject relevant to the content of the message.

Attachments: File attachments can be documents, pictures, video or sound files sent along with your message.

Body: The main body of the e-mail contains the message itself.

Retrieving E-mail Messages

Once you have received an e-mail message, it will automatically be located in your Inbox.

New e-mail messages will always appear in your Inbox and can be instantly recognised by their bold text. To retrieve your document, simply click once with the left mouse button for it to appear in the preview pane, or alternatively, double-click the message item in order to view it in a separate window.

Reading E-mail Messages

Once the message appears in its own window, the message subject will appear in the title bar of the message window. The message contains its own menu bar and toolbar. By selecting the **Previous** and **Next** buttons, other messages in the selected folder can be read.

To close the message window once read, click on the cross at the top right of the window (the **Close** button).

Deleting E-mail Messages

E-mail messages that you no longer wish to keep in your inbox can be sent to your **Deleted Items** folder. ───────────────────────── Deleted Items

Simply highlight the e-mail you wish to delete by clicking once with the left mouse button and pressing the **Delete** key on your keyboard, or by clicking the **delete icon** on the toolbar. ─────────────────────────

The item has now been sent to the **Deleted Items** folder, but it can still be retrieved and has not been completely deleted. In order to completely delete a message item from Outlook Express, access the deleted items folder, select the item you would like to delete and press **Delete** from your keyboard, or click on the delete icon from the toolbar.

Forwarding E-mail Messages

Open the message you wish to forward and select the **Forward** button on the Standard toolbar.

Here you are required to enter the address of the recipient in the **To:** text area. If you wish to add any further comment, type above the existing message. Click **Send** to forward the message.

Opening Attached Files

E-mail sent with an attachment will arrive in the Inbox with a small paperclip icon to the left of the message.

To have a look at the attachment, double-click the e-mail subject title to open the message in a separate window.

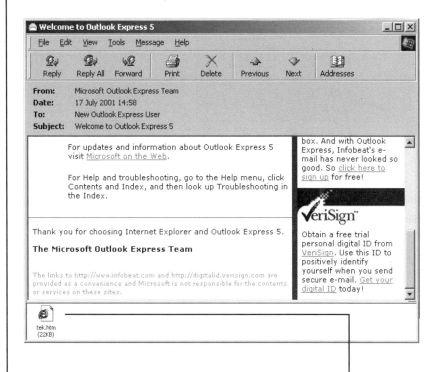

At the foot of the window should appear the **attachment** as a file icon; double click to open the attached file.

Attaching Files To E-mail Messages

Once you have composed your message including the e-mail address of the recipient and subject heading, select the **Attach** icon from the Standard toolbar.

From the subsequent **Insert Attachment** dialogue box, click on the drop-down arrow from the **Look in:** section to allocate the file you wish to attach to your message.

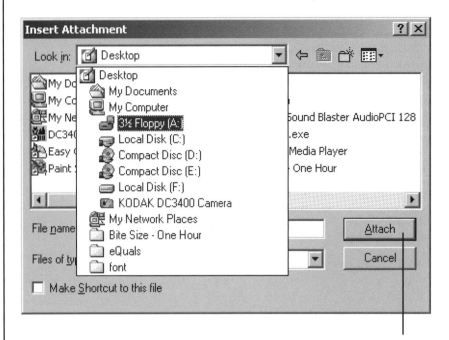

Once you have located the file, select it and click the **Attach** button.

The file will now be inserted under the subject section of the Outlook Express window. Click **Send** to 'post' your e-mail.

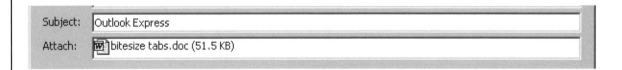

Saving And Printing E-mail Messages

When you save an e-mail message, Outlook Express will automatically send it to your Sent Items folder for future reference.

To save an e-mail, click **File** from the e-mail message window then **Save**.

Your message will not have been sent, but will now be located in the **Drafts** folder.

To retrieve your message, click on the **Drafts** icon from the folder list. Double-click the Subject title of the e-mail in order to view your message.

Printing An E-mail

To print an e-mail message from your Inbox, first select the e-mail you require with a single click of the left mouse button, then click the **Print** icon from the Standard toolbar.

<u>Shutting Down E-mail Program</u>

To close the Outlook Express application, either click on the cross on the top right hand corner of the Outlook Express window,

or

Click on **File**, **Exit** from the menu bar to close the program, or
File, **Exit and Log Off** to close the program and disconnect from the Internet.

	Task 11/60.	E-mail Tasks (Supplementary Pack).

T A S K	1. *Close the open e-mail program.*

APPENDIX

Glossary of Terms

©Tektra TEKIE1RP1102

FTP	File Transfer Protocol	A code system designed for the uploading, downloading and general transfer of any ASCII or binary file amongst servers and clients. Programs, data files and web pages are transferable using this system. It is too cumbersome for regular surfing page access.
Gigabyte		1024 Megabytes.
Hardware		Any tangible computer machinery. For example; sound cards, modems, monitors (screens), keyboards, mice.
Home page		A web site's central page from which others are accessed by hyperlinks. Modem home pages are designated index.html on each site.
HTML	Hypertext Mark-up Language	A simple text and picture layout programming language intended for the design of web pages.
HTTP	Hypertext Transfer Protocol	A code system designed for efficient web page download to clients. The usual Internet transfer protocol (http://).
Hyperlink		A clickable text phrase or picture visibly distinguished on a web page and fundtioning as a 'trapdoor' through which to access other sites or pages.
Internet		The entire system of computerised telegraphy used to exchange web site information, e-mail and other files over the international telephone network.
ISDN	Integrated Services Digital Network	A bi-channel digital protocol for copper wire, dial-up telephone lines. 64Kbps Baud telephone network.
ISP	Internet Service Provider	An agency which brokers Internet services between web users, specifically those with client stations. For example; AOL, Freeserve, BT Anytime.
Keyword		A highly relevant word of natural language used by a search engine to identify interesting websites, which are then reported to the human searcher.
Kilobyte		1024 bytes.
Local access number		A reduced rate, or freephone, dial-up telephone number for cheap use of a narrowband ISP service.
Megabyte		1024 Kilobytes

Meta search		A 'search amongst serach engines' where several search engines are made to scan for and pool interesting websites.
Modem	Modulator demodulator	A solid state electronic machine for converting analogue to digital signals and vice versa. It is needed because the public telephone system uses analogue, or wave-profiled, electrical signals, whilst computers use digital, or pulse-profiled, electrical signals.
Narrowband		A slow Internet access service involving intermittent dial-up single-line telephonic access.
Search engine		A computer program designed to find and list the URLs of interesting websites.
Server		A web page and other file-keeping and transmitting computer, traditionally a heavy mainframe. Any computer can, however, be programmed to behave as a server.
Simplex		Carrying electric signals in only one direction, eg conventional TV broadcasts.
Software		Any coded recording such as programs or data files. For example; spreadsheet programs, browsers and word processor documents are all software recorded on disk or tape hardware.
URL	Universal Resource Locator	The unique address of a given Internet page. The URL is made up of domains, For example, http://www.madeup.com
Virus		A self-propagating computer program sent secretly to "infect" other data systems. Viruses may be harmless, inconvenient or highly-destructive.
www	World Wide Web	A very large, public Internet domain designed for easy, open public access. World Wide Web URLs take the form http://www.etcetera